Common Core Lessons & Activities:
Civil Rights

By Carole Marsh
Published by Gallopade International, Inc.

Printed in the U.S.A. (Peachtree City, Georgia)

TABLE OF CONTENTS

G: Includes Graphic Organizer
GO: Graphic Organizer is also available 8½" x 11" online download at www.gallopade.com/client/go
(numbers above correspond to the graphic organizer numbers online)

Black Codes & Jim Crow

Read the text and answer the questions.

After the Civil War, Southern governments passed laws to limit the rights and activities of freed slaves. Known as "Black Codes," these laws were an attempt to keep African Americans under the control of white southerners. Black Codes gave African Americans some rights like the right to get married or own property, but mostly, black codes limited their rights. For example, blacks were not allowed to testify against whites in court, vote, or serve on juries. They could only hold certain types of jobs, and they were even told how late they could stay out at night.

Northern states were outraged at how freed blacks were treated. The Civil Rights Act of 1866 and the passage of the 14th Amendment put an end to Black Codes. However, Southern governments found other ways to discriminate against African Americans. They passed "Jim Crow" laws that lasted from the late 19th century until the mid-1960s.

Jim Crow laws set up segregation in all walks of life. They separated blacks from whites in public places, including schools, restaurants, movie theaters, hotels, and even doctors' waiting rooms. These separate facilities were supposed to be "separate but equal"—but they were far from equal. African American facilities were inferior and not well supplied. Jim Crow laws became a central issue of the Civil Rights Movement.

1. A. Define discriminate as it is used in the text.
   B. Define segregation and provide an example.
   C. Define inferior. Provide a synonym and an antonym.
2. Explain the relationship between Black Codes and Jim Crow laws. In what ways were they similar? In what ways were they different? Use a Venn Diagram to organize your answer.
3. According to the text, were Jim Crow laws fair to African Americans? Explain your answer with evidence from the text.
4. Use online resources to learn where the term "Jim Crow" originated. What does the term reveal about those who first came up with it?

Jim Crow Political Cartoon

Look at the political cartoon and answer the questions.

Courtesy of Wikipedia

1. What does the "Jim Crow Car" symbolize?
2. What does the "Car for White Folks" symbolize?
3. Explain the message of this cartoon.
4. What do you think the cartoonist's opinion is on the issue of "separate but equal" facilities for blacks and whites? Cite evidence to support your answer.
5. In your opinion, is this cartoon effective? Why or why not?
6. Explain the relationship between this cartoon and the overall Civil Rights movement.
7. Imagine you are an African American living in 1950 under segregation. Use the picture above as the basis for a short essay explaining the concept of "separate but equal." Edit and proofread your essay.

13th, 14th, and 15th Amendments

Read the text and answer the questions.

From 1865 to 1870, Congress passed the Thirteenth, Fourteenth, and Fifteenth Amendments to the Constitution. These amendments declared slavery illegal and gave African Americans citizenship, equal treatment under the law, and the right to vote.

After the Civil War ended, members of Congress worried that Lincoln's Emancipation Proclamation would not guarantee freedom for slaves. Therefore, Congress proposed the Thirteenth Amendment, which abolished slavery when it was ratified in 1865.

In 1868, the Fourteenth Amendment was ratified, granting African Americans U.S. citizenship. The amendment prohibited any state from depriving citizens of their right to due process, meaning a fair trial as a citizen of the United States, as well as equal protection under the law.

The Fifteenth Amendment, ratified in 1870, gave African Americans the right to vote. For a brief time, African Americans were able to vote freely and elected many African Americans to office in the first few years after the Civil War.

However, problems were on the horizon. Although a great step forward for civil rights, the amendments did not solve all the problems faced by African Americans after the Civil War.

1. According to the text, why was the Thirteenth Amendment necessary?
2. Define due process as it is used in the text.
3. Explain the relationship between citizenship and equal treatment under the law.
4. What is the common theme among the three amendments?
5. Compare and contrast the freedom of African Americans before and after these three amendments, which were known as the Reconstruction Amendments. Working in groups, prepare a computer presentation. Present your work to your class.

Civil Rights Vocabulary

Use the dictionary and other resources to fill in the Vocabulary Word Map for each of the words or terms below. Give as many examples, nonexamples, and characteristics as possible.

Vocabulary:

- boycott
- civil disobedience
- civil rights
- discrimination
- integration
- march
- nonviolent protest
- riot
- segregation
- sit-in

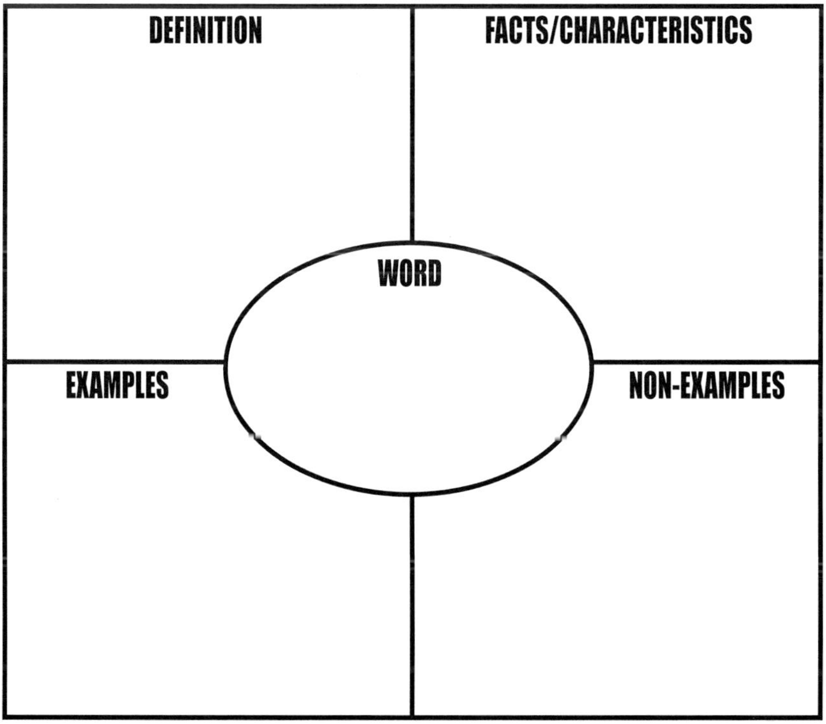

Plessy v. Ferguson & Brown v. Board of Education

These texts are paraphrased excerpts from famous civil rights cases Plessy v. Ferguson and *Brown v. Board of Education.*

Read the texts and answer the questions.

In all public transportation, as in railway and bus companies, this state shall provide "equal but separate" areas for the white and colored races. On each train, white passengers will occupy the front while colored passengers will sit in the coach, or separation can be made by using a divider. In all cases, passengers must do as instructed by the bus driver or train conductor regarding seating.

Plessy v. Ferguson (1896)

Segregation of white and colored children in public schools is harmful to the colored children. Separate African American schools often have poorer quality textbooks, fewer school supplies, and fewer teachers than in white schools. Therefore, African American children feel inferior to whites and have no motivation to learn. Segregation laws are a significant problem to the education and academic development of African American children. African American children would have better opportunities attending the same schools as white children.

We conclude that, in the field of education, "separate but equal" is not fair and will not be allowed. Separate educational facilities are inherently unequal.

Brown v. Board of Education (1954)

1. Summarize the main idea of each text.
2. How does the opinion about "separate but equal" differ between the two legal decisions?

Writing Prompt:

Imagine you attend a segregated school. Predict how *Brown v. Board of Education* will change your life. What problems might you encounter?

Effects of Discrimination

Complete the graphic organizer with the effects related to discrimination and civil rights.

Cause:	Effect:
African American and white children attend segregated schools.	
African Americans are not allowed to sit in the same area as whites on buses and trains.	
Martin Luther King, Jr. gives the "I Have a Dream" speech	
Oliver Brown, and many other African American parents file a lawsuit against the Board of Education in Topeka, Kansas.	
Civil Rights activists in Birmingham fought for desegregation of transportation and restaurants.	
Many people took action to stop desegregation.	

Peaceful Protest Tactics

Read the text and answer the questions.

Civil Rights leaders used many types of protests to support their cause. The most effective protests were nonviolent protests in the form of boycotts, sit-ins, and marches. African American leaders such as Dr. Martin Luther King, Jr., used nonviolent protests. Many Civil Rights leaders saw nonviolence as the only way to bring positive attention to their cause and create lasting change.

From 1955 to 1965, nonviolent protest was effective in causing change. Sometimes, nonviolent protesters disobeyed the laws they felt were unjust without fighting or causing people to get hurt. In Alabama, people protested against segregated city buses by boycotting, or refusing to ride them. Black college students began "sit-ins," where they sat down in "white-only" diners. If told to leave, the students stayed seated, quietly and respectfully, until they were forced to leave, often by police.

Peaceful marches were another form of nonviolent protest. But peaceful marchers were often treated with violence and hate. On one famous march from Selma to Montgomery, Alabama, police tried to stop the peaceful marchers with tear gas, clubs, and whips. These televised marches of police violence caused many Americans to speak out about the need for change.

1. Define the phrase nonviolent protest as used in the text.
2. Describe an example of a nonviolent protest including who, what, when, where and why.
3. What was the purpose of using nonviolent protest?
4. Based on the text, what can you conclude about the motives of protestors who participated in sit-ins?
5. Predict what might have happened if African American protesters had used violence during marches, sit-ins, and boycotts.
6. Compare what you know about America today with America as described in the text to answer the question, "Were nonviolent protests effective in the Civil Rights Movement?"

Civil Rights Organizations

Do research on civil rights organizations and their methods to fill in the graphic organizer.

SCLC	SNCC	NAACP
↓	↓	↓
Methods	Methods	Methods
↓	↓	↓

Common Goals

Civil Rights Quotations

Rewrite each quotation to complete the chart. Use the completed chart to answer the questions.

Civil Rights Movement quotations:	What each quotation means to me:
"I would like to be remembered as a person who wanted to be free… so other people would also be free." *— Rosa Parks*	
"…The United States has been called the melting pot of the world. But it seems to me that the coloured man either missed getting into the pot or he got melted down." *— Thurgood Marshall*	
"Nonviolence is a powerful and just weapon. It is a weapon unique in history, which cuts without wounding and ennobles the man who wields it. It is a sword that heals." *— Martin Luther King, Jr.*	

1. Who are the speakers? Use online research to write a short biography of each speaker. Proofread and edit your work.
2. What can you infer about Rosa Parks' character from her quotation?
3. Thurgood Marshall's idea of America as a melting pot of all races means that all races are treated equal, but he says the colored man "missed getting into the pot." Explain the meaning of this statement.
4. What words does Martin Luther King, Jr., use to paint an image of nonviolence in your mind?

PRIMARY SOURCE ANALYSIS

Separate Facilities

Look at the photograph and answer the questions.

Courtesy of Library of Congress

1. At first glance, what is your eye drawn to? Why?
2. What concept does this photograph illustrate?
3. What can you conclude about the date of this photograph? What evidence supports your conclusion?
4. Describe three inferences you can make about the community where this photograph was taken.
5. Imagine you are the boy at the water fountain. Write a short narrative about the photograph.
6. Go online to find images of segregated facilities in the U.S. during the mid 20th century. Work in groups to prepare a computer presentation of the images you collect. Present your work in class.

Complete the graphic organizer by identifying the key issues and change agents of the Civil Rights Movement. Write issues and agents in each circle and explain the significance of each on the lines next to it. Then define Civil Rights in your own words.

Key Issues

____
____
____

____
____
____

Civil

Definition

____
____
____

____
____
____

Change Agents

Rights

People

Methods

Events

Legislation

READING INFORMATIONAL TEXT

Little Rock Nine

Read the text and answer the questions.

Although opposed by many people, the desegregation of public schools was a major achievement for the Civil Rights Movement. The 1954 *Brown v. Board of Education* case declared segregated schools to be "inherently unequal." The U.S. government ordered that schools be desegregated. This order allowed black and white students the opportunity to attend schools together. Unfortunately, the first few years of desegregation were a time of much racism and violence in schools.

In Little Rock, Arkansas, the governor refused to allow nine high school students to attend Little Rock Central High, which was an all-white school. When the "Little Rock Nine" arrived for school on September 4, 1957, angry protestors and the armed Arkansas National Guard refused to let them inside. President Eisenhower ordered that the children be admitted, and federal soldiers walked them into the school. During their first year, the Little Rock Nine were bullied and physically hurt by many of their classmates. Only three of the original Little Rock Nine graduated from the high school.

In 1962, James H. Meredith registered at the University of Mississippi. An angry mob formed to prevent his enrollment and attacked the federal marshals protecting him. Although Meredith became the first African American to attend a Mississippi public university with whites, his struggles were far from over. Like the Little Rock Nine, he faced daily discrimination in school.

1. Define the word desegregation by giving a(n):
   A. Synonym   B. Antonym   C. Example
2. Why did the U.S. government order desegregation of schools?
3. What is the main idea of the text?
4. Why did the Arkansas National Guard refuse to allow the "Little Rock Nine" to enter the school?
5. Compare and contrast the two examples of school integration in the text.
6. Why do you think only three of the Little Rock Nine graduated from Little Rock Central High? Cite evidence to support your response.

Voices of the Civil Rights

Use what you know and online resources to complete the information for each influential person in the Civil Rights Movement. Tell, "Who am I?" and "What did I do?"

People:	Who am I?	What did I do?
Booker T. Washington		
W.E.B. DuBois		
Rosa Parks		
Martin Luther King, Jr.		
Malcolm X		
Thurgood Marshall		
Jackie Robinson		

Montgomery Bus Boycott

Read the text and answer the questions.

Before the Civil Rights Movement, public bus transportation in the South was segregated. African Americans had to ride in a separate section at the rear of the bus. They were also required to give up their seat to white people if the bus filled up. White bus drivers often treated them rudely. Sometimes black passengers had to pay up front, get off the bus, and re-enter through the back door. Some drivers even drove away before they could get back on!

On December 1, 1955, Rosa Parks, already sitting in the colored section, refused to give up her bus seat to a white male. She was promptly arrested. Supporting Rosa Parks' action, the Women's Political Council organized a boycott of all segregated buses for December 5, 1955. The Montgomery Bus Boycott was born!

Martin Luther King, Jr., quickly became the spokesperson for the boycott, giving public speeches and leading demonstrations. He strongly supported using nonviolence at all times. The boycott lasted just over one year. On December 20, 1956, a federal court required desegregation of public transportation in Montgomery.

In many ways, this boycott was the first major event of the Civil Rights Movement. During this time, Martin Luther King, Jr., became a national leader for African American civil rights.

1. A. Use a dictionary to define boycott.
   B. Infer the meaning of spokesperson from the text.
2. Explain the significance of the Montgomery Bus Boycott to the Civil Rights Movement's fight against segregation.
3. What conclusions can you draw about Rosa Parks' beliefs by examining her actions on the Montgomery bus?
4. Use the text to number the following events in chronological order:

_____Martin Luther King Jr. becomes a national leader for the Civil Rights Movement.
_____Rosa Parks is arrested.
_____Montgomery Bus Boycott ends with the desegregation of public transportation.
_____African Americans are required to ride in the back of public buses.
_____Montgomery Bus Boycott begins on December 5, 1955.

MAP ACTIVITY

Freedom Rides

Use the text and the map to answer the questions.

In 1961, groups of white and black Americans went on "Freedom Rides" throughout the South. Their purpose was to see if new federal laws outlawing segregation at interstate bus terminals were being followed. The first two Freedom Ride buses left Washington, D.C., on May 4, 1961, to arrive in New Orleans on May 17. After splitting ways on May 14, the "Freedom Riders" were stopped by angry protesters in Alabama. Many riders were beaten and jailed.

Freedom Rides Route Map:

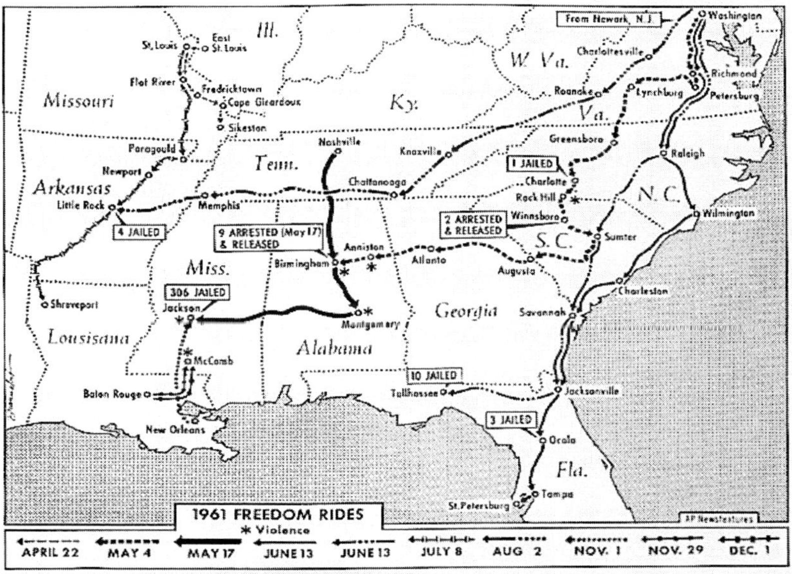

1. What was the purpose of the Freedom Rides?
2. What is the purpose of this map? List the types of information this map is designed to provide.
3. What is indicated by a ✳ on this map?
4. What can you infer about the people who participated in Freedom Rides? List at least three inferences and explain your reasoning.

March on Washington

Analyze the picture and text to answer the questions.

This picture was taken on August 28, 1963, during the March on Washington for Jobs and Freedom. Representatives from many labor and religious organizations marched alongside supporters of the Civil Rights Movement. Of the approximately 300,000 marchers, 75 percent were African American and 25 percent were non-African American.

Courtesy of National Archives

1. List some of the civil rights the protesters wanted.
2. How important are the posters in getting across the message here?
3. Infer the mood and tone of the people in this photograph. Cite evidence to support your opinion.
4. What message do the protesters give by the clothing they wear?
5. Describe the relationship between African Americans and non-African Americans in the March on Washington. Cite both text and image.

PRIMARY SOURCE ANALYSIS

"I Have a Dream" Speech

This text is an excerpt from a speech given by Martin Luther King, Jr., on the steps of the Lincoln Memorial during the March on Washington.

Read the speech excerpt and answer the questions.

1. Go back to Mississippi, go back to Alabama, go back to South Carolina, go back to Georgia, go back to Louisiana, go back to the slums and ghettos of our northern cities, knowing that somehow this situation can and will be changed. Let us not wallow in the valley of despair.
2. I say to you today, my friends, that in spite of the difficulties and frustrations of the moment, I still have a dream. It is a dream deeply rooted in the American dream.
3. I have a dream that one day this nation will rise up and live out the true meaning of its creed: "We hold these truths to be self-evident: that all men are created equal."
4. I have a dream that one day on the red hills of Georgia the sons of former slaves and the sons of former slave owners will be able to sit down together at a table of brotherhood.
5. I have a dream that one day even the state of Mississippi, a desert state, sweltering with the heat of injustice and oppression, will be transformed into an oasis of freedom and justice.
6. I have a dream that my four children will one day live in a nation where they will not be judged by the color of their skin but by the content of their character.
7. I have a dream today.

1. What repetitive phrase sets the tone for the excerpt? What does this phrase mean in the context of the speech?
2. What is the main message of the speech?
3. Explain the meaning of "rise up" in section 3. How is this effective?
4. Which section refers to an end of segregation? Is Martin Luther King, Jr.'s example meant literally or figuratively?
5. What is implied by "even the state of Mississippi" in section 5?
6. Analyze the word choices used to describe Mississippi in section 5. What does MLK accomplish with his description?

Malcolm X & MLK Ideology

Martin Luther King, Jr. and Malcolm X were major figures in the Civil Rights Movement. Both men wanted freedom and an end to segregation, but their views on violence were very different.

Read the quotations and answer the questions.

> Returning violence for violence multiplies violence, adding deeper darkness to a night already devoid of stars… Hate cannot drive out hate: only love can do that.
>
> –Martin Luther King, Jr.
>
> *Where Do We Go from Here: Chaos or Community?* (1968)

> I am for violence if non-violence means we continue postponing a solution to the American black man's problems just to avoid violence.
>
> –Malcolm X
>
> *The Autobiography of Malcolm X*

1. Compare and contrast the points of view.
2. Do you agree or disagree with the opinion expressed by MLK? Why or why not? Write a new quote that would match MLK's philosophy.
3. Do you agree or disagree with the opinion expressed by Malcolm X? Why or why not? Write a new quote that would match Malcolm X's philosophy.
4. As a class, discuss and debate your responses to the questions.

Civil Rights Act of 1964 & Voting Rights Act of 1965

Read the text and answer the questions.

The Civil Rights Acts of 1964 and the Voting Rights Act of 1965 were great achievements for America's Civil Rights Movement. After many years of demonstrations, protests, and speeches, these two laws were passed to protect African American' civil rights.

Although slow to create change, the Civil Rights Act paved the way for racial equality in America. It outlawed segregation in public places like swimming pools, schools, and public libraries. Additionally, it made discrimination in the workplace illegal and ended discrimination in businesses such as theaters and restaurants.

The Voting Rights Act (1965) reinforced the Fifteenth Amendment passed during Reconstruction, 95 years before. For too long, African Americans had been denied voting rights by the use of unfair poll taxes, literacy tests, and intimidation when registering to vote. The Voting Rights Act made all forms of voter discrimination illegal. Taking effect right away, the act was highly successful in raising the number of African American voters.

1. Use a dictionary to define discrimination
2. Explain why discrimination was an obstacle to the civil rights and voting rights of African Americans.
3. List a cause and effect of the Civil Rights Act of 1964.
4. List a cause and effect of the Voting Rights Act of 1965.

Writing Prompts:

What can you infer about the 15th Amendment based upon the passage of the Voting Rights act of 1965? In a well-organized response, explain how the two are related.

"Great accomplishments are never the result of one person's labor." Write a well-organized paragraph supporting this statement.

Voting Statistics

Use the data in the table to answer the questions.

Voter Registration Rates (1965 vs. 1988)

	March 1965			November 1988		
	Black	White	Gap	Black	White	Gap
Alabama	19.3	69.2	49.9	68.4	75.0	6.6
Georgia	27.4	62.6	35.2	56.8	63.9	7.1
Louisiana	31.6	80.5	48.9	77.1	75.1	-2.0
Mississippi	6.7	69.9	63.2	74.2	80.5	6.3
North Carolina	46.8	96.8	50.0	58.2	65.6	7.4
South Carolina	37.3	75.7	38.4	56.7	61.8	5.1
Virginia	38.3	61.1	22.8	63.8	68.5	4.7

1. What is the purpose of this table?
2. Summarize the significance of the data.
3. A. In 1965, which state had the lowest percentage of registered black voters?
   B. What can you infer about racial discrimination in this state in 1965 compared with other states.
4. Explain "Gap" as identified in the table.
5. How does the gap in black and white voters in 1988 compare with the gap in 1965?
6. Why is the 1988 Gap for Louisiana negative?
7. The Voting Rights Act of 1965 is commonly called the "single most effective piece of civil rights legislation ever passed by Congress." How does this table support that statement?

Civil Rights Events

Put these events in chronological order on the graphic organizer.

Plessy v. Ferguson: "Separate but Equal"	Civil Rights Act passed	Rosa Parks arrested	Voting Rights Act passed	March on Washington for Jobs and Freedom
14th Amendment	Montgomery Bus Boycott	First Freedom Ride	15th Amendment	*Brown v. Board of Education* decision

Major Civil Rights Events:

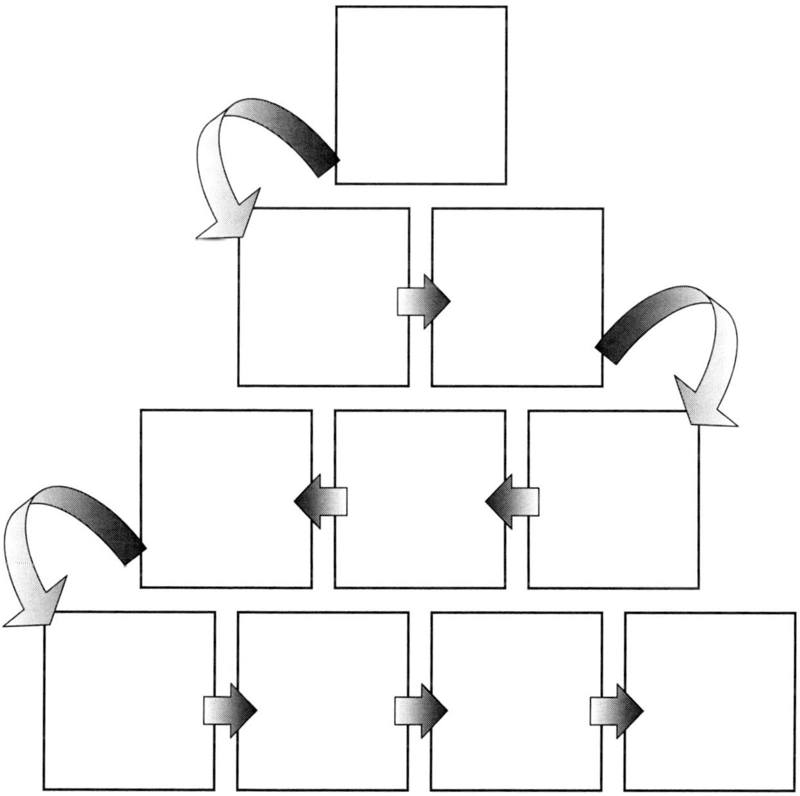

Correlations to Common Core State Standards

For your convenience, correlations are listed page-by-page, and for the entire book!

This book is correlated to the Common Core State Standards for English Language Arts grades 3-8, and to Common Core State Standards for Literacy in History, Science, & Technological Subjects grades 6-8.

Correlations are highlighted in gray.

(Highlighted numbers shown in **bold**.)

PAGE #	READING *Includes:* RI: Reading Informational Text RH: Reading History	WRITING *Includes:* W: Writing WHST: Writing History, Science, & Technology	LANGUAGE *Includes:* L: Language LF: Language Foundational Skills	SPEAKING & LISTENING *Includes:* SL: Speaking & Listening
2	RI RH . **1 2** 3 **4 5** 6 7 8 9 **10**	W WHST . 1 2 3 **4** 5 6 **7** 8 9 **10**	L LF . 1 2 3 **4** 5 **6**	SL . 1 2 3 4 5 6
3	RI RH . 1 2 3 4 5 6 **7** 8 **9 10**	W WHST . 1 **2** 3 **4 5** 6 7 8 9 10	L LF . 1 2 3 4 5 6	SL . 1 2 3 4 5 6
4	RI RH . **1 2** 3 **4 5** 6 7 8 9 **10**	W WHST . 1 **2** 3 **4** 5 **6** 7 **8 9 10**	L LF . 1 2 3 **4** 5 **6**	SL . 1 2 3 **4 5 6**
5	RI RH . 1 2 3 **4** 5 6 7 8 9 **10**	W WHST . 1 2 3 4 5 6 7 8 9 10	L LF . 1 2 3 **4** 5 **6**	SL . 1 2 3 4 5 6
6	RI RH . 1 **2** 3 4 **5** 6 7 8 9 **10**	W WHST . 1 2 **3** 4 5 6 7 8 9 **10**	L LF . 1 2 3 4 5 6	SL . 1 2 3 4 5 6
7	RI RH . 1 2 3 4 **5** 6 7 8 9 **10**	W WHST . 1 2 3 4 5 6 7 8 9 10	L LF . 1 2 3 4 5 6	SL . 1 2 3 4 5 6
8	RI RH . **1 2 3 4 5** 6 7 8 9 **10**	W WHST . 1 2 3 4 5 6 7 8 9 10	L LF . 1 2 3 4 5 6	SL . 1 2 3 4 5 6
9	RI RH . 1 2 3 4 5 6 7 8 9 10	W WHST . 1 2 3 4 5 6 **7 8 9 10**	L LF . 1 2 3 4 5 6	SL . 1 2 3 4 5 6
10	RI RH . **1 2** 3 4 5 6 7 **8** 9 **10**	W WHST . 1 **2** 3 **4 5 6 7 8 9 10**	L LF . 1 2 3 4 5 6	SL . 1 2 3 4 5 6
11	RI RH . 1 2 3 4 5 6 **7** 8 **9** 10	W WHST . 1 2 **3** 4 5 **6 7** 8 9 **10**	L LF . 1 2 3 4 5 6	SL . 1 2 3 **4 5 6**
12-13	RI RH . 1 2 3 **4 5** 6 7 8 9 **10**	W WHST . 1 2 3 4 5 6 7 8 9 10	L LF . 1 2 3 4 5 6	SL . 1 2 3 4 5 6
14	RI RH . **1 2 3 4 5** 6 7 8 **9 10**	W WHST . 1 2 3 4 5 6 7 8 9 10	L LF . 1 2 3 4 5 6	SL . 1 2 3 4 5 6
15	RI RH . 1 2 3 4 5 6 7 8 9 10	W WHST . 1 **2** 3 **4** 5 **6 7 8 9 10**	L LF . 1 2 3 4 5 6	SL . 1 2 3 4 5 6
16	RI RH . **1 2** 3 **4 5** 6 7 8 9 **10**	W WHST . 1 2 3 4 5 6 7 8 9 10	L LF . 1 2 3 4 5 6	SL . 1 2 3 4 5 6
17	RI RH . **1 2** 3 4 5 6 **7** 8 9 **10**	W WHST . 1 2 3 4 5 6 7 8 9 10	L LF . 1 2 3 4 5 6	SL . 1 2 3 4 5 6
18	RI RH . **1 2** 3 4 5 6 **7 8 9 10**	W WHST . 1 2 3 4 5 6 7 8 9 10	L LF . 1 2 3 4 5 6	SL . 1 2 3 4 5 6
19	RI RH . **1 2** 3 4 5 6 7 **8** 9 **10**	W WHST . 1 2 3 4 5 6 7 8 9 10	L LF . 1 2 3 4 **5 6**	SL . 1 2 3 4 5 6
20	RI RH . 1 2 3 4 **5** 6 7 8 9 **10**	W WHST . **1** 2 3 4 5 6 7 8 9 **10**	L LF . 1 2 3 4 5 6	SL . **1** 2 3 4 5 **6**
21	RI RH . 1 2 3 4 5 **6** 7 8 9 10	W WHST . 1 **2** 3 **4** 5 6 7 8 9 **10**	L LF . 1 2 3 4 5 6	SL . 1 2 3 4 5 6
22	RI RH . 1 2 3 4 5 6 7 **8** 9 10	W WHST . 1 2 3 4 5 6 7 8 9 10	L LF . 1 2 3 4 5 6	SL . 1 2 3 4 5 6
23	RI RH . 1 2 3 4 **5** 6 7 8 9 **10**	W WHST . 1 2 3 4 5 6 7 8 9 10	L LF . 1 2 3 4 5 6	SL . 1 2 3 4 5 6
COMPLETE BOOK	RI RH . **1 2 3 4 5 6 7 8 9 10**	W WHST . **1 2 3 4 5 6 7 8 9 10**	L LF . 1 2 3 **4 5 6**	SL . **1** 2 3 **4 5 6**

For the complete Common Core standard identifier, combine your grade + "." + letter code above + "." + number code above.

In addition to the correlations indicated here, the activities may be adapted or expanded to align to additional standards and to meet the diverse needs of your unique students!